THE BOOK OF SHADOWS

# THE BOOK OF SHADOWS

*New & Selected Poems*

CARLOS REYES

LOST HORSE PRESS
Sandpoint • Idaho

# ACKNOWLEDGMENTS

I am especially grateful to my publisher, Christine Holbert, to my friends and fellow poets, Christopher Howell and Vern Rutsala, and to my wife, Karen Checkoway. Without them this book would have never seen the light of day.

I would like to thank the Oregon Arts Foundation's Individual Artists Fellowship (Poetry), which allowed me to return to Ireland in 1983. In addition, I gratefully acknowledge the Yaddo Corporation, the Fundación Valparaíso (Mojácar, Spain), the Heinrich Boll Association (Achill Island, Ireland), and Joshua Tree National Park, for the residencies that gave me inspiration and the opportunity to devote my time entirely to writing.

A number of these poems have appeared in the following anthologies:

*A New Geography of American Poets, Long Journey, Poetry and Prose Annual, Portland Lights, Portland Poetry Festival Anthology, Prescott Street Reader; Rough Places, Sierra Songs & Descants, Hunger and Thirst, Beloved on the Earth, Spotlight 2* (Dublin, Ireland), *The Stoney Thursday Book* (Limerick, Ireland).

Acknowledgements are due to the editors of the following publications in which some of these poems first appeared:

*Antioch Review, Ar Mhuín na Muíce (On a Pig's Back), Caffeine Destiny, Calapooya, Chadakoin Review, eye-rhyme, Ergo, Fireweed, Gumbo, Heliotrope, Hubbub, Lettera* (Cardiff, Wales), *Litmus, Local Earth, Matrix, Mid-American Review, The Minnetonka Review, Mississippi Mud, Neon, One Mind* (Tokyo, Japan), *Pebble Broadsheet* (Limerick, Ireland), *Poet Lore, Portland Magazine, Rain City Review, Redaction, Salt River Review, Solo, Take Out, The Burnside Review, The Northern Review, The Oregonian, The Other Side, The Portland Review, The Review, The Willamette Bridge, Willow Springs*.

The selected work is taken from the following books:

*The Shingle Weaver's Journal* (Lynx House Press, 1980).
*Nightmarks* (Lynx House Press, 1990).
*A Suitcase Full of Crows* (Bluestem, 1995).
*At the Edge of the Western Wave* (Lost Horse Press, 2004).

*Book design by* Christine Holbert.
*Poems selected & arranged by* Christopher Howell.
*Cover art:* Reverse of a painting, "Murakami Gates," by David Luckert.
*Author photo by* Karen Checkoway.

Library of Congress Cataloging-in-Publication Data

Reyes, Carlos, 1935-
    The book of shadows: new & selected poems / by Carlos Reyes.
        p. cm.
    ISBN 978-0-9800289-6-6 (alk. paper)
    I. Title.
    PS3568.E883B66 2009
    811'.54—dc22

                                    2009037348

## BOOKS BY CARLOS REYES

### POETRY

*The Prisoner* (Capra Press, 1973)
*The Shingle Weaver's Journal* (Lynx House Press, 1980)
*At Doolin Quay* (Lynx House Press, 1982)
*Nightmarks* (Lynx House Press, 1990)
*A Suitcase Full of Crows* (Bluestem, 1995)
*At the Edge of the Western Wave* (Lost Horse Press, 2004)

### TRANSLATIONS

*Puertas abiertas / Open Doors* by Edwin Madrid (Eskeletra, 2000)
*Poemas de la isla / Island Poems* by Josefina de la Torre (Eastern Washington University Press, 2000)
*Obra poética completa / Complete Poetic Works* by Jorge Carrera Andrade (Casa de la Cultura Ecuatoriana, 2004)

# CONTENTS

## SHADOWS | A SEQUENCE (2005)

## *from* THE SHINGLE WEAVER'S JOURNAL (1980)

*from* NIGHTMARKS (1990)

*from* A SUITCASE FULL OF CROWS (1995)

*from* AT THE EDGE OF THE WESTERN WAVE
(2004)

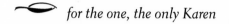 *for the one, the only Karen*

NEW POEMS (2006–2008)

She used
just one

of the empty
bottles

as a rolling
pin

when she baked
bread

for his return
like Penelope wove

she baked and if
he did not come

she fed the loaves
to seagulls

As is known
the rolling pin

whether glass
or wood

makes a weapon
she kept it close

in her apron
just in case

the waves
brought someone else

# SHOT GLASS

With the bottom
of the thick glass

he works chancres
into the mahogany

the heel of his hand
rests on what

germs reside there
though the bar

is wiped clean
and shines in the

light of the afternoon
sun stabbing through

the smoky glass
The bar is filthy

half the lives
who come here

are lost in the
dirty wiping rag

the other half
in the porous wood

plank where they
have left

—scratched there
with coins' serrated edges—

their scars

# THE HEEL

It's called:
the last few drops

in the bottle
If Moses tapped

your heel stone
bruised

viper struck would
all those years

of eighty proof
gush forth?

The molasses-
colored bottle

who opened it?
How is it

that its eight ounce
capacity

can hold a whole life?
How many

bubbles, molecules rising
does it take

to make the genie
that escapes

into the always
arriving night?

# WORK IN A COFFIN FACTORY

The wages were low
I didn't work there long

Between jobs
as a construction laborer

My union was out on strike
so rather than scab

I scoured the want ads:
the job was only one of two

I ever found in the paper

Each morning I came in
after the free roaming Dobermans

were put back in their kennels
and swept up their leavings

Mixed in with cedar shavings
I likened the aroma to sacrificial incense

so I never crossed the transom
into the other room

never looked a coffin in the eye

*—for Julie Checkoway*

Framed in the oval
window of a door
a long woman in black
talks on the telephone
distances, looks out
on an empty street
in a city in the desert.

She is at the expectant
edge of the Great Salt
Lake, has grown tired
waiting, she is about to
pass through beveled
glass into the light
this September.

## MARACA MAN

He is happy
(his other pair of shoes
will be ready on Saturday)
but he is also afraid
to leave his maraca shoes
with George to fix them,
afraid they'll lose
their sound, rhythm.
He almost has it down,
is almost ready
to dance through the window
to merengue with the barefoot man
who walks by
if he ever shows up without his dog.

# TRADING A BUCKET OF WATER
## FOR THE MOON

The tin pail I drop
down the well
shatters the moon.

As the bucket fills
it gathers up
silver fragments.

Sent only for water
I am happy to carry home
the shimmering moon.

I run to the house
proud of my catch, eager
to show my mother.

As I hurry I splash
pieces of silver
on the sun-dried earth.

From the porch
she sees this
as broken mirrors, bad luck

Fears the worst, the curse
of seven nights
of moonless sky.

Last time it was
a bag of stars I spilled
along the dusty road.

## BETWEEN THE FIRST AND SECOND SHOE DROPPING

He takes his last drink
kisses his last girl
eats his last meal
chokes on the bone
of the fish caught
thousands of miles
away and brought
to the market a few
blocks from here.

He walks his last mile.

Here on the edge
of my world
I sit waiting
for the other shoe.

I choose a square
of rough paper cut
from a sea
of trees, take up
a pencil for him.

He draws his last breath.

Because the coffin
was widened to accommodate
corpulence

the bat-winged
box would not fit
through the front door.

Because they could not
wake the dead man
beneath the moon
or under the pale sky.

Because the men
of the town land
spent days, widening
the portal.

Because the soul
got tired of waiting,
one afternoon
when the workmen
were having tea,

the coffin lifted off,
flew away in the first dust
storm in thirty years.

Away, away over the sea
toward the horizon's
eyebrow of clouds.

The sun winked
like a lighthouse
strobe

across the beetle
black shel-
lacked vessel escaping.

UNCOLLECTED POEMS
(1980–2005)

I

Until wine spills over the silver rim of sky's bowl,
Until our eyes are red as night's foolish ink,

Until the wind's music will have no more of song,
As we fight to keep our sea legs, until Polaris dances.

# I KISS YOU NOW ACROSS THE MANY HUNDREDS OF MILES THAT SEPARATE US

—Marina Tsvetayeva
*No One Has Taken Anything Away*

As suddenly as the page turns
the trail presents two choices.

The fork that looks to be the right one,
should he choose it, would surely be wrong.

With no coin to flip does he look for the sun
behind the blanket clouds, behind the ridge,

listen to the trees
or turn his face into the leaden rain?

Behind him an icy roaring stream;
the bridge disappears in mist.

In his ears the ocean breaks far away.
A double ended wooden boat capsizes

and drifts—its captain overboard
long since given up swimming home.

Even if the book is closed tightly
and put away, the boat's still drifting.

In the next chapter or the one after,
someone at the crossroads will have to choose

or sit down on the log to rest and fall asleep

while the boat drifts to him.

Up the trail in the window a lantern flickers,
a fireplace lights up the cabin

where someone reads the book,
clothes on the chair, drying

while the lighthouse casts its dim strobe
on an upturned double ender drifting.

# THE FIRST TIME I SAW PARIS

It was raining
as we sat
beneath the Arc
d'Triomphe

Ate bread
from across
the boulevard
and cheese

Where
chains prevented
the Two Horses
the Peugeot
the Dauphine
from passing
under the arch

Where French honor
—the army—arrived
at exactly 2 P.M.

and the rain
marched off
to another world

Just past midnight eight hours from Madrid,
the other passenger who speaks only Arabic

thinks he has bought a ticket to Almería.
*But it says Mojácar* insists the driver, stops

pushes the Arab from the bus.
The driver, whose looks could demand papers,

asks only to see my ticket again, says
to the darkness, to me, *I hate people*

*who don't know where they are going* . . .
Repeats it to make sure I've understood

before I fall asleep . . . while the bus,
a beetle with flashing eyes,

rides the spine of a glistening black snake
on down the grade, toward Turre.

Guitars and voices crack the night.
Gypsy moths dance on the face of the moon.

# POEM

*— for Lawson Inada*

The backdrop of the camps,
a tall canvas reaches the sky
streaked carmine, volcanic
ash particles in the atmosphere,
a forest fire in the mountains.

At sundown in the foreground
you introduce your father,
take him aside confidentially.

Smiling he tells you, a small boy,
what your part in this will be,
essaying various flute-like instruments,

apologizes to you, plays
a few notes, the call of an unknown bird,

smiles with kindness
at the rivulet of disparate notes.

You are saying *This is internment*
as your arm sweeps the stage
behind you, the vast auditorium

where the audience turns program notes,
searches the red afternoon, impressed
only by the fire burning the sky.

A jazz suite: lachrymose notes,
the smoky night comes on, a tinkling

of raindrops, the last
note of a rare bird's song, you say

*This is the camps*

# LORCA'S SHIP

*—for Greg Simon*

Where one expects
*The Export Queen*

Or *The Pacific Trader*
Tied up at the grain elevators

In Portland harbor
Instead the *Luna Verde*

Where riverine
Creatures scurry

Up ratlines in pale light
To the green moon

And sailors
From Cartagena

Lean against
Hatch covers

Sing gypsy ballads
In a swirl of chaff

Smoke Gitanes
In the cloud

Of explosive grain dust
Laugh

At the danger
The night

The stars
Embedded

In black hills
To the west

*. . . Dreams pour into your pillows.*

—Mark Strand
*The Coming of Light*

My pillow is too hard.
Are you sure you don't have mine?

> I didn't know we had
> individual pillows . . .

We could trade but I wouldn't want
you to get my dreams . . .

> That's very interesting
> Me getting your dreams . . .

> I said I didn't want to trade
> because you might catch my germs . . .

I don't care what you said . . .
Give me your pillow, give me your dreams!

When you are at your bath
and I come in to talk to you

to wonder at your nakedness —
you have left the towels

scattered like fallen silk
robes — you ask me, accusing,

did you step on them?  Today
standing in the tub, listening

to the water drain as I dry,
two things occur to me:  one

I am using your towel
and two, that you are gone.

Will anything of you sloughed off
stick to me, as I dry myself,

surely some essence, some scent
remains there on the towels

you have used.  My mind drifts,
considers a Caribbean love potion —

could I drink a glass of your
bath water? If you drank

a glass of mine, would you become
enchanted, would it make you crazy

for me? The towel you used
last week is around my shoulders,

not at all like your arms, your warm
hands.  The wind from the east now

is warmer, will dry me quickly . . .
Through the open door, the sad damp

towel, on the tile floor, blue
fading in the morning sun, edges unraveling.

—*for Claudette Reyes*

Though I have never seen
Such fields, I like the metaphor

It reminds me of Claudette,
Whose father was from Nicaragua

Claudette of the mountainous, delicious
Chocolate sundaes, I loved her

For the exquisite political protests
She dreamed up, fueled by

Her hearty dislike of gringos
When Eisenhower came to

The Hemisphere talks in the '50s
Her idea was to get all the *Panameñas*

To line the route of the motorcade
Throw their American G.I. babies back

Into the passing convertible, into the
Arms of the secret service, and into the open

Arms of the smiling Great White Father

# CARDBOARD BOAT IN OPEN WATER

*They should never talk of light who won't*
*risk waking in cold dawn with the blunt face*
*of some strange love, unwrapped and snoring*
*in the grinding stillness of a foreign room*

—Frank Stewart
*Harbour Shadows*

The four of us walked past
the bullring hoping for more
beer, but the kerosene lamp
at the closed and barred door
had long since guttered out.

So we danced like bears
toward Araceli's habitation
and took to our cardboard
boat of a bed to make love
but fell asleep instead.

Voices in a foreign accent half-
woke me to sunlight dancing
along the obsidian sharp horizon
of a kitchen knife she threatened
her *compañero* with . . .

Told me that love's hour
was past, that I should softly
say goodbye to my sleepy friend
before the neighbors peeked in . . .

Before the *guardia* arrived
I was out of the room up
the alley to cool shadows.

At the San Francisco Bullring
while I waited for the chiva bus
the local population made its way
toward church and the *Misa
de los perezosos,* mass for late risers.

I smoked my last crumpled Viceroy
and with my left hand shielded my eyes
from Sunday morning's blinding light.

# MEMORY

So what if the *Luna Azul*
was really the *Gruta Azul*

forty-five years ago, and
memory didn't get it exactly right?

So what if the blue sign
has faded, the building

boarded up?  That evening
outside the whorehouse

the tall skinny cab driver
threatened the four of us

with a baseball bat
he extracted

from the trunk
when we refused to pay.

In the dim moonlight
as if he had just come up to bat

he said simply, in his best
West Indian English "Now

just which of you gentlemen
wants to be first?

# WALKING INTO THE HEART OF PANAMA

Evening coming, young
    and afraid

I have wandered into
    the sudden dark

of the jungle. Unsure of
    which way to go

I bump into the wrong tree,
    black palm spines.

Sweat in each puncture
    mixes with blood,

one or two needles left
    beneath the skin, the sting

reminds me I am
    loveless, lonely, lost and

thirsting, remembering
    what I learned,

to cut beneath the spines to the heart
    of the heart

hold the juicy warm pulp
    to my face.

All fear and callowness
    whispering away.

Beneath the jungle's
    erotic call

I dance to the castanets
    of exotic insects, sing

with the nightbirds
    for all I'm worth.

II

*—for Pablo Neruda (1904 - 1973)*

Yes, I know exactly where I was—
on a bus near the Spanish frontier
between Andorra and Barcelona.
The man ahead of me reading
headlines proclaiming to the world
the death of one of its great poets.

With the bottle of cheap rum
rolling around beneath the seats,
put there to avoid customs,
not found by the Guardia Civil,
I drank a toast to you, Pablo —
Neftalí Reyes Basoalto—Neruda.

I bought this small sheaf—your last
Words—in a kiosk on Las Ramblas
and strolled with the crowds.
At a cafe I savored the sweet
strong coffee, the lasting word,
the title *Aún.*

One small word, *Yet,* swims
in the ship's phosphorescent trail
during my sleepless wake for you
on the moonlit sea all the way
to Mallorca at sunrise.

## IN THE FALL

I walk the dangerous edge
of damp graveled roads
the perimeter of aging forests
the changing leaves
the gold instead of green
twirling in a colder wind.

How I enjoy
the smell of wild apples
beginning to turn cidery
with bitter frost
crabapples like dim lanterns.

Hoping for one more day
before the rains arrive
I walk down the leafy lane
to see a break
in the clouds and bright
sun once more

before winter tightens
its jaws around the trees
before the grey pulling
clouds suffocate the wind
before lakes, rivers and seas
fall from the heavens
drown every green thing
fading all green all gold
to dull and papery pale.

# EVERYTHING IS METAPHOR

*—for Jonathan Johnson*

Outside the cabin: wind, rain drenching
the grass, the trees. A roar waking me
is a narrow creek
pulled swiftly downhill by its gradients
to Clark's Fork village.
Each pine
needle but a leaf
each wet blade
only grass, yes
each stone slab a step down
but leading only to a mossy lane.
A retaining wall
holds but empty shoulder-
high iron restraining rings,
nothing more sinister
than tethers for mules
their hoof prints long erased
by rain, their steaming breath
gone to mist
above the trees.

# A FOSSIL FERN, 1944

The man who brings the ice
brings coal to our porch
in burlap bags. Not today.
We could be those children
scrounging along the tracks
for bits of coal fallen from gondolas.
Our last piece of coal, I want to keep it,
with its delicate fossil of a fern exposed.
My mother has no trouble
deciding between beauty or comfort in December.
In a room where you can see your breath
she breathes: dust, dirt, black coal, ashes . . .
But fuel not fern is the final word
thrown on the dying fire where it begins to glow,
finely drawn pencil lines, finally taken to flame.
Yet I watch until my eyes burn,
all the heat I get, that and night's thin blanket.
Old clothes, coats the things
I would gladly trade to save the fern.

After two weeks of Basic Training
came the night for faked combat
crawling the infiltration course,
for ambush along
darkened trenches,
singing trip wires,
for blinding phosphorus,
for the voice of Tokyo Rose
seeding the suspicion
blossoming in my heart:
was my girlfriend
back home unfaithful?
Still waiting?

I snake along
the belly
of the muddy night
beneath barbed wire.

I have no girlfriend
but Rose, some other
war's scratchy voice
waiting up ahead . . .

Here live rounds slice to rags
the darkness overhead.
Red erratic tracers
stitch back together
this unending night over

the new fatigues,
each future wave.

# POEM FOR TOMAS TRANSTRÖMER

If you examined
the broken glass
atop the walls
how many drops

of dried blood
would you find
on the glass?
On your own wrists?

And how many
glasses of fine wine
came from the broken
bottles? Where
are the drinkers?

I want to know
why the trespassing
or escaping red rose
dared to climb
up over the wall

after the glancing
sunlight walked
carelessly among
those diamond chips,

after the moon
scratched and bleeding
let fall its drops of blood
or red petals as it rose.

I

The ship had gone down
in the blackness we drifted
in oily warm water
clinging to our life
vests calmly talking
to one another

I woke / fell
back asleep

II

We were still
in the tepid sea
though quieter

Out of the darkness
came the voice

*This is the captain*
*speaking . . .*
*in a few minutes*
*it will be daylight*
*then the sharks will come . . .*

# ESTATE

Each piece of paper
each leaf each
breath left

or scent inhaled
from a piece of clothing
in a green and yellow box
from Brazil that says

*"Entrega Urgente"*
*"Cuidado Frágil"* . . .

I spend the weekend
at estate sales trying
to determine if this
is how we measure

our lives, by what's left behind
to sell to strangers—the box
marked "free." Untouched
as though unclean . . .

In the end does it matter
if the prints of our passing
ends up as rummage?

We sniff the air inside
the garages and houses
of strangers, judge
their lack of taste,
their sentiments.

But when the chattels are our own?
How reluctantly we part
with these traces

This plastic bag,
the scent the piece of clothing
in it carries, we are sure we know it
before we seal it up again
in the carton labeled

"... Urgent" "... Fragile"

That scent a breath
still alive
as we take it briefly
into our lungs.

## A FEW DAYS BEFORE SEPTEMBER

I am under
a pale finger-
nail paring moon,

jarred from my reverie
by an intensely silver
almost wingless propeller-
driven airplane

roaring
across the zenith
of my pleasant
Sunday morning,

awakening the still
dead, those sleeping, those
with hangovers,
those with morning after

regrets,
those who thought
today was their day
and nothing more,

oblivious
to the dying of time
that this might be the last
most beautiful day
of summer

when all
the natural world
is on the verge.

Beauty gives way
to grim survival
in a corner
less lit by the sun.

## ODE TO COINS

You know the coppery flavor
of pennies
so you swallow a nickel
just to know its taste.

The coin
has little distinctive flavor
as it goes down, down

Jefferson's head
on one side
E Pluribus Unum over
Monticello
on the other . . .

That night
you put your rotten tooth
under the pillow
expecting
a reward, a return
on your investment,
the American dream
of waking to paper money.

But the dream turns:
somewhere Jefferson's face
is lying in a pile of shit, yours.

You are asking him
if it tastes different
on the other side
of the coin
in Monticello.

He winks
becomes the Brave
face on the buffalo nickel.

He knows the taste of blood
the taste of defeat
the taste of death.

And he knows the smell
of cooking fires laid well
with buffalo chips.

On the other side of the nickel
the last free ranging bison,
captured in a circle of silver.

Yes, he knows
what buffalo shit tastes like,
knows too what the dust
of buffalo chips tastes like,
ground
to powder
beneath ponies' hooves
on the other side of the nickel.

He too is captured
in a ring of silver.

The buffalo
is still here
in real life
behind a fence
off the nickel.

Brave
so far disappeared,

the coin
his face is on

only collectors have
or people
who live in countries

where old American coins
still circulate,

like Cuba
where I saw him last.

When the other prisoner
incises the hash mark

whether it represents
one hour, one day
one year . . .

His cell mate
pays no attention
to the hieroglyphics

the ogham marks
on the limestone wall
but wonders

in this place
empty of every
thing but two

unwashed bodies
the occasional
rat visitor, lice

Where the nail
came from: a cross?
does it carry

tetanus germs
from manure
from some barnyard?

would it
make
a weapon, a

means of
suicide
escape?

Suddenly he is
covetous of his cellmate

wants the nail
wonders what
it tastes like

longs to touch
it with his
tongue

taste its red rustiness
taste the rain
barrel residue

In the night
oblivious
to the moon

He watches
over the
other man

dreams
of killing
his cellmate

possessing
the treasure
nail

He wakes
crying
for the nail

tastes nothing
like he dreamed
but like

the old
iron pennies
from the crock
behind the stove
at his grandmother's

His cellmate
is still alive

The nail
hidden
in the waistband

creasing, leaving
no doubt
a faint

impression
in his beer
belly

the man
he watches
never talks to

# FOR A SISTER LOST IN WATER

You must still be here
in the universal rising mist of morning.
Where the eye, the sun who
walks this way, searches even here for you
as I stand on stone cliffs,
as the rapids swirl around me.

The aroma, the taste of resin,
the wet logs I sit on remember you,
a picture gone as quickly
as the restive red crawfish
scuttling to shadows of an overhang
at the bottom of the pool
where fingerlings nibble
at the edges of our ancestors.

*The salmon—falls, the mackerel—crowded seas*
*fish flesh or fowl, command all summer long*
*whatever is begotten born and dies.*

—W.B. Yeats
*Sailing to Byzantium*

Where two rivers meet, say
Nehalem and Salmonberry,

where long disused
rusting train tracks

come descending
out of dark tunnels

from places long abandoned
like Cochran,

where the spotted fawn
raises its head with

no fear of hunters,
takes tentative steps,

its spots replicating
patches of snow

left among salmonberry
brambles, nods its head

up grade or down slope.
The jack salmon

knows no such hesitation
follows the gradient

upstream, follows his
cannibalistic bent, eats

the coming generations.
Behind him the big male salmon

swimming fast in pursuit,
diverts his zigzagging foe

from the nest of eggs
buried in shallow sand.

I have hooked the jack
breaking the chain.

He's black on
the riverbank, will

eat no more salmon eggs,
will  be food instead

for crows, hawks, eagles
and vultures.

I have killed the jack
God that I am

I will not eat him
he is too dark

even for smoke,
too near death.

I abandon  him
and trudge back

up the railroad grade
back to ghost logging

towns, back to gravel
roads cut into hillsides

away from where
the snow is melting

into sweet water, into
threads, rivulets

and creeks that inexorably
draw upstream

—stronger than moon tides—
all swimmers to death and birth.

Where she lives
it's three days ago

Where she plays
her violin

the still tree
still has leaves

Where soap
bubbles turn

into a myriad
of octagon shapes

knotted into seines
cast and lost

in morning fog
burnt up in the rising sun

Where the tide
rises in footsteps

fast clicking high
heels castanets

Where she dances
in the wind

Where flying fish
nest in the trees

with
small finches

Where silken
threads of nests

come undone
signifying

the end
of every ochre world

When did
she come here

and why
She was not invited

staggered
down the shallow stream

her feet bare,
her skirt rent

When did
she awaken

in the house
at once

roofed with palm
with thatch

When did
she decide

to stay here

When did
the children

leave singing
When did they

begin crying
in the dark woods

When will
the moon

come back
to her

green children

Our love world:  that sweet forbidden fruit
was a hard green apple split in half
when she picked me up at the plane.
Seven days of drinking in Berkeley
gave me wisdom I thought, like Solomon.
*What about the kids* she asked?
*We'll split them down the middle.*
*Two apiece I suppose? No,*
*I mean split each child down the middle*
Solomon wise, Solomon style.
*You're drunk* she says, her wisdom.

I think of them on days I pass by offshore.
If I look closely I see people waving,
blowing kisses, saying
*see the boat out there, it's him!*
They wave more madly,
I wave back frantically, not knowing
if they really see me.

The nearest harbor is miles
or years away . . . When I get there
they are all grown up, have children
of their own and I have changed,
as strange to them as their mother
is to me leaving me wondering,
did we live together
in that land before children where
love at first sight struck me blind?

The binoculars are no help.
The trees are different, exotics
unknown to me, the wind the sky

a history of blank pages no matter
how I try to read them
through salt spray, lenses fogged.
My heart wrapped in down
keeps away the bitter wind
at sea, in January.

# THE FOGHORN BREAKS HIS HEART

The old man
walks-shuffles, wooden
lobster pot on his shoulders.

Fog follows him
up the rocky grade
toward Cemetery Hill.

The lobster pot's
slats are barnacled,
as calloused as
the old man's
sausage fingers
and ham fists.

The rib-like
slats of the half moon
trap broken . . .

The cage of salt air,
low-tide seaweed,
he struggles to carry
like a treasure chest
up the hill from the dock
away from the boats
heeled over
on the tidal flats.

# IN THE HARBOR OUR SLEEP RUSTS
## QUIETLY

---

—Sheenagh Pugh
*Sailors*

Rust buckets, the old freighters
listing half full of water
about to spill.

A Spanish friend came to Portland
aboard an old C-2
oxidized outside and in,
pumped and raised given new life
with Greek registry.

His job aboard welding the leaks
keeping her afloat.

But when the ships stay in port
they rock like old men
on the porch, weeks of stubble
on the chin
half asleep.

Beards at the waterline
in fresh water too long, these vessels
will never cross the bar again,

like my friend who came ashore
years ago

who neither bid me fair voyage
or waved goodbye when I sailed

into the dangerous sea breaking
over relation—
ships of divorce . . .

He never spoke to me again.

Ay! My friend . . .

# THE ROAD AWAY FROM THE SEA
## IS DIFFICULT

The man pulling the boat
up the highway on a trailer
the tow line cutting
into his shoulder is Nikos

who flees from the angry ocean
where fishing is bad where
he almost drowned

His partner Elpenor even more disgusted
with life at sea is two miles up ahead
his burden lighter by far an oar
over his shoulder

At road's edge near the gates
of a cemetery he waits
shaking his fist at passing motorists

He is watched over by an angel
in marble whose left forearm
and wrist are mysteriously missing

The statue's disconnected
fingers support the uplifted
trumpet which will announce
the arrival of Nikos and the boat

Against the oak Elpenor
leans the oar its heft sinking
into the soft grass and waits

blue fisher's cap in hand
as the sun a leaden hundred drachma
coin drops into sea mist
behind the mountains

On any day of the week
widows covered in dusty black
line up in the chapel to receive communion.

If it's Wednesday
young householders drawn
by the aroma of fresh bread
wait in line for the bakery to open.

But the baker has long since
put the iron gate over the doors,
put in place the shutters and
gone home to hearth.

The moon hangs full
in the evening sky,
the poets drunk as the summer
stars line up.

They have their tongues out,
waiting for someone
to place the moon wafer there.

# HE WOULD HAVE SAID

*—for Walter Hall*

it is the rims
of dirty glasses

in half light,
the moon

scarred mahogany
reveals

moons over moons
over years.

He looks up
and out

the window
into the dark

sky as black
as the long bar.

He would
have said

you are all
wrong

those marks
are scars

of all the lives
passed here.

All the smiles
miles of seduction

smiles revealing
bad teeth

delightful early
flirting laughing.

Late blind
drunken ribaldry

guffaws like
roaring waves,

beer foam
left upon the glasses,

sleepers left
upon the shore.

Where's the moon
of romance now?

he would have said.

# VERÜCKTE JUTTE

She clips the lawn
with ordinary scissors

and keeps her vigil
over empty meadows

from daybreak until dark
from her vantage on the porch.

She hides behind the newsprint barricade
now that fall rains have come.

In the backyard, for all we know,
she uses a common salad fork

to make the huge, perfect shock
of hay that cures then rots.

The flashlight, her imperfect moon,
tells her all the fields are scissor-mown.

But darkness comes and hides the street,
the hitching ring is rusting on the stone.

 III

*—for Ron Taylor*

The man walks
out of his living

room into the painting.
He crosses the arched

(or crosses the aisle
and sits down to watch

the movie
of a certain)

stone bridge
where he meets Van Gogh.

The painter hurries
past as if to say

Can't you see
I'm busy.

The sun is shining,
the sky so blue

I have so much to paint
and so little time . . .

Then suddenly
the moon the painter's ear

fits perfectly in the sky:
the last piece

of a jig-saw puzzle.

The man near
the head of the line

turns to face us
licks stamps

his tongue out
like someone

taking communion.
Up on the wall

Christ on the clock
arms outstretched

says quarter to three.
That his right hand tries

to raise itself, that
his left arm slumps

is an illusion.
The waterclock

has stopped,  the
last seconds dry

on his pale wrists.

# WHISKEY BOTTLE / ROLLING PIN

I watched her that day
take his pint of Old Crow,
place it on the fence post
in plain view of the neighbors
and aim rocks at it
until she broke that vessel to smithereens,
contents vaporizing to summer sky.

She kept an whiskey bottle,
her only rolling pin.  It stood there
On the table as she made bread,
a reminder, as the afternoon sun
winked, as he sat reading *The Mail*.

# THE IRON BOAT'S OAR

*—for Seamus Heaney*

In late summer my father brings back
a straight piece of hickory from the country,
sharpens his pocket-knife and begins whittling.

He spends weeks on the front stoop
that white piece of wood across his knees,
shaving and planing,
shaping a smooth handled oar.

Every night, home from the garage,
he takes the piece, aims it toward the light,
checks its true, begins his task

whittling between sips of ice tea
dreaming of corn liquor, pausing
to wipe his brow with his railroad kerchief,
then planing and shaving until he loses the light.

I ask him what it is for, fearing
the paddle. He
smiles—a rare thing
for him—and says it's for the boat.

November and the first hard frost comes
even to the city. We head out
to Conway, to my grandmother's.

A fire of oak is blazing in the yard
the huge iron kettle on its three tiny toes
over the roaring heat and a tripod raised with pulley
for dunking hogs in scalding water . . .

It isn't the popping of dry sticks in the fire
we don't want to hear, but that other sound
before the hog drops in its tracks,
or the squeal if the bullet misses.

On the backseat of the '39 Essex, the oar—wrapped
in clean white cheesecloth—rests on mohair
until the butchering ends and the rendering begins.

Then my father brings out the oar
to stir the cracklings until they melt into fat
in the huge black cast iron pot he calls the boat,

stirring and stirring until the fat is rendered
poured off, cooled and hardened into pure white lard.

The black iron boat that would hardly float the Osage,
is leaned up against the oak, its perfect oar
that took so many weeks to fashion

thrown onto last coals
to blaze up and disappear in smoke
and ashes of the frosty afternoon.

I would run to the open fire and rescue
the oar now seasoned, tested and cured with pig fat
and sweat from my father's hands.

But something unknown to me
requires his ritual carving,
shaping a new oar every year.

My father tries to explain it all
to my mother, she never understands . . .

Muffled voices in the basement,
heavy boots walking over my head

as the black suits go through the attic.
Without explanation

they take the house apart:
dump drawers, strip beds,

empty closets, rip
boxes, tear open pillows

in an explosion
of down, a spit of snow

that covers everything;
cupboard doors left a-swing,

the family bible rifled . . .
Like the prairie wind

they come and go, head
up town to my father's shop

and pick him up. Forgery they say, hot
checks.

# DARK JAKIS

In the small photographs
he's always near the dark edge
almost behind a tree—never
the focus but his presence
draws the eye.

Mysterious, his hat
Caribbean,
out of place.

Dark Jakis shadows
the family watching
at the picnic.

He never leaves his place
in the corner
of every photograph,
never speaks and when
his brothers and sisters refer to him,
they call him everything
but Jakis.

Like so many I wonder,
who my forebears were.
Racial memory or coincidence,

a strange expression breaks
through, swims to the surface,
sends me running for the dictionary.

A bit of language:

when making soda bread
an ingredient
known only to my mother, some magic
added to the mix—

lumpy, sour and Celtic—
clabber comes back to me.

# THE BASEMENT ROOM

*—for Rachel Kathleen Reyes-King*

She scratches
initials and date
into the fresh cement.

With chalk line
we mark off and
begin to build

the bedroom
in  the basement.
Much the way

my father taught me
when I  was her age,
I show her how

to grip the hammer,
drive sixteen penny nails,
construct the stud wall.

When I return there
I worry around on cool, darkening concrete,
inspect the square penciled "closet"

where boxes list unopened,
where my pride and hers—
the blue and yellow bird feeder

she made herself
from shingles—fills slowly
with flaking whitewash.

A fading blue double line,
bare studs, rib cage
around the dusty air:

the room
unfinished.

SHADOWS | A SEQUENCE (2005)

of a land
where there were no shadows

though the sun shone
in a cloudless sky

His theory was
that in some war or other

they were all taken prisoner
and marched away

You see their remnants
in the black and white stripes

of prisoners uniforms
in old movies

# AN ECOLOGY LESSON?

The shadows
in single file

one morning
marched out into the lake

and back
On shore

each one
picked a single pine

to stand behind
that's why

all the shadows
have disappeared

That's why
the loggers

have cut down all the trees
along the lake

stick shadows
become confused

and cry
put their hands

in front of
their faces

become
crucifixes

lose themselves
in hilly old cemeteries

# HOW SHADOW LOST FACE

A very small boy
is impressed

with his shadow
he talks to it

though in whispers
The shadow

yells at him
Why are you whispering!

The boy thinks
it's only the wind

A shadow can fish
If you have seen

what happens
when clouds get

between the sun
and water on the lake

You'll know what I mean
the fish go crazy

If shadow
has a bucket or a net

or can cup his hands
he will catch many fish

## AMORES

Two shadows
fall in love. No

Two clouds
can fall in love

They can meld
join they can reproduce

They can easily
disappear

behind other clouds
Jealousy is not

an unusual characteristic
of shadows but

unknown to humans
shadows have a great penchant

for revenge

There are days in Alaska
when there are no shadows

That is why often
in winter the Yupik quietly

walk through their villages
lanterns held high

calling *chamai chamai*
The White man thinks

it is only
wind through the snow drifts

It is the Yupik trying
to convince the shadows

to return

# NO SHADOW LEFT BEHIND

Have you ever seen
small shadow children

getting on a yellow school bus?
No. But you have often

seen them waiting
along the road where the bus comes

Sometimes
found off the edges

of certain concrete
buildings

You know how
sharp those shadows are

They cut
you know they can

You have seen them
cut a man

or a dog
in two

# DO SHADOWS GROW OLD?

Do shadows age?
A Greek poet says yes

When they are young
shadows are black as octopus ink

As they age
they grey become

diffuse

The shadows
dancing around the edges
of a campfire
are joyous

(the faces watching
don't understand this)

(they look fearful)

The shadows are happy
they know they can outlast
wood that
they may soon get some rest

They are not threatened by distant stars
but are wary
they know the full moon
can keep them awake all night

# WHO SAYS SHADOWS DO NOT DREAM?

If they could
what would they dream of?

Shadows though often
have restless nights

When will the sun come up?
Will it rain instead?

Why did they turn off
the lights in the big picture

window of the house
across the street?

Or let the street lamp go out?
Such worries keep

the shadows turning
and tossing all night

Sleep deprivation causes them
to hallucinate

have bags under their eyes
but they definitely

do not dream

Yes, shadows go to war
No history book has

established that there
was ever a war without shadows

There is always for example
the clichéd shadow of death

But the shadows know
it is not a cliché

For though they do not enlist
many of their number are chosen

for that duty
But there are also shadows

who protest every war
As is to be expected

the shadow warriors outnumber
the protesters

# THE BIRDS AND THE BEES AND SHADOWS

No one has ever seen
a shadow give birth

(said the Greek poet)

though many have seen
small shadows grow larger

around the middle
I for one have heard

female and male shadows
on the street

talking about sex

Shadows have never
heard of birth control

I think they like
the intimacy of the reading lamp

They will keep you company late at night
as you read

If you fall asleep
without turning off the lamp

You can be sure shadow
will be there keeping you company

all through the night

Somehow in the morning
your pages have turned

You're not on the page
where you left off reading

Or shadow has fallen asleep too
and carelessly let your book

fall to the floor
beside your bed

# SHADOW DOES TIME

I know you know
shadow hides

sneak thieves cutpurses
aids and abets

all kinds of criminals
He witnesses crime

but will never rat
on anyone

Shadow hates jail
when he is in solitary

beads of sweat form
on his forehead

He prays to the moon
for freedom

*from* THE SHINGLE WEAVER'S JOURNAL
(1980)

## I

He looks at his hands
small for a man
of his size,

the rivers there
go nowhere

begin, are lost
on the same plain.

A poor map
with which to start
the journey, his feet
are too small.

The fog moves in
on him
like a blanket
left out to air and
dry, then rained on.

How he longed
to be away.

## II

Ridges and valleys
a kind of scapulamancie
(without the scapula) the
game played

solitaire
as he sits on the
cedar

log and counts
the ridges on
the fingers of both

hands: ten ridges, ten
valleys thinking
about the journey
about what lay
beyond the ten

ridges, imagining thirty people
with sixty hands
a forest of snags

the sea fog spilling over.

Someone forgot
the champagne, brought
instead polluted water
from the Willamette.
There is no arm strong
enough to break the coke
bottle and the bow
crumples like balsa.
The captain is
drunk in Valhalla—
a tavern on Burnside Street—
where he has shanghaied
a crew from among the winos.
The charts in his back
pocket are written
in classic Transylvanian & crushed
between his tremendous ass
and the oak bar stool.
Thursday when he sobers
up a coast guard captain will
tell him the ship
has been launched and floats
free, last reported
five hundred miles south
west of Cape Blanco
& drifting.

# THE DREAM

The trees would not stop after the seven hills
where the smoky purple ridges are stacked up
one behind the other and you could count them
until your eyes grew tired . . . and maybe a meadow
where the widest road was a deer trail
a few inches wide and a thousand miles long
and where what you thought was smoke
from a cabin or a mill was morning mist rising
and where what you thought was smoke
from a cannon
was morning mist.

Fools we came
here at 2 A.M.
standing on the ruins
of Fort Stevens buried
in the sand to wait.
5 A.M. & it is up
this tricky channel of
shifting bottom sands, the
way ships must come
from the sea
through the grave —
yard into the Columbia, up
to Portland. Hardly
before we are awake
small fishing boats slip
silently
down the mist
into the Pacific.
Then dim light
ghosts come: destroyers,
the destroyer escorts, the LST,
one submarine
black, hard
silhouette passes
war (pale grey)
ships go past
in a long quiet heart beat.

*Hammond, Oregon*
*June 10, 1969*

I offer a poem freshly killed,
a junkie who would do anything,
a thief becoming a thief,
an adulterer going to bed,
a rapist going to rape,
an unnatural act about to begin,
a leech too fat to walk back to Akron,
my casket hand carved by me
from cheap pine and painted
with black Shinola.

Uptown, at the barbershop
the pool has been formed:
each man has put in his
four bits and picked the day
the old car under the bridge
will fall through the ice.

The woolen mill at Old Town
has been struck for almost a year;
production is not curtailed
          —there is always
            someone who needs
work.

     *Ice on the Stillwater is breaking up*
*and the men of the village are busy*
        *building*
        *new bases*
*for the brass cannons*
    *that face*
*the river.*

# TWO FOR PABLO

## I

When I run out of blue
I use red, said Picasso
which explains a lot
of things, say, for example
why the harlequin has
one blue ball, one red
but does not explain
that quizzical look
in Pablo's eyes as he
stares between his legs.

## II

A blue sun drops
behind forty miles of
smoke painted by Picasso.
Imagine this is Portland,
Oregon. The forest is burning down,
the last four lines are false,
you have sneezed on your mustache,
your last friend has just said
                              goodbye.

Hidden entrances, where
hillsides open
into rooms of the
limestone caves
often echoing
chambers & flowing
rivers beneath the earth.

Saturdays we spend
exploring in the dark,
brave in the stories
we tell on Monday.

We always carry a ball
of twine—short pieces of
string saved for months
to unwind as we go in, so
we can find our way
out—& candles to
light in the dark.

We hear the rushing
water of the river, deep & wonder
about eyeless fish & we are
scared of snakes & the warmth / damp
ness & whatelse we do not know.

We never bother to mention
we never go far enough
to unwind the ball of twine,
that we never dare light the candles.

Home was a streetcar up on blocks,
in a tourist court called Uncle Tom's
Cabins. On Saturday we went up town.
Once my father took me
to the auditorium, pointed
and said: That's Joe Louis
heavyweight champion of the world.
When I think of 1943, the war
and Salina, Kansas, I see
the regiment of black soldiers
—laces broken on their white
leggings—marching up the road.

Rodríguez the Mexican couldn't speak
Spanish.  And Roger the Cherokee
had to fight to prove he wasn't
a Panamanian. & Clutch Riley the Texan, telling
Preston, "Man, it don't make no difference
when you go home on leave, you see my folks
you hear?" & Bob Young who married a Cuban
singer, dancer and bar girl
in spite of the objections of the C.O. and the Rabbi.
& Preston whispering to me he's going
down to Chorrillo, where he can find a woman, and I'd
better stay here with Riley and the others.
& Rico the West Indian bartender, toeing the mark
for his bosses. & Cholo, full-blooded
Choco Indian, mopping the floor.
& the barmaids inside the bar
& the blue mooners at the tables
& the whores in the street
& the fairy waiting in the shadows
whispering at passing G.I.s
& Clutch Riley saying to Preston
"Man, it don't make no difference . . ."

*Panamá*
*1955*

# PYRITE

The man who first settled this area
came across the bar in a long-boat
and lived through the first rainy winter
in a hut fashioned in the bowels
of a Western red cedar.

He must have traded with the Indians
who brought gold down from a secret
mine in these mountains of the Coast Range.

At Stone's Camp in a shake cabin
under dripping fir boughs I spent one
winter exploring, looking for that mine
and prospecting for gold in the streams.

My father said you never
find gold unless it is in hard rock.
I found a woman
to walk the woods and river banks with:
iron pyrite, in these mountains
of shale.

From most anywhere in Tillamook County
you can see the landmark: Gold Peak.
Here, at its base in Stone's Camp,
the peak itself is not visible. Below the cabin
is the river where my little sister almost drowned and I,
too, the coward, almost. They once hung my father
by the waist from the bridge.
After a night over the mist and icy water
he was sober. Long winter nights I spent
here talking to my sister and listening
to the water roar under the bridge, the short wave
radio and the rain falling through tall firs.
Here, on this island of trees saved from a fire
that burned everything,
I found the muddy roads, through trees
and along the rivers. My second boat
—a thirty foot gill netter—I left here: smoke
curling up from red cedar through
the timber, blown by the southwest wind
away from the sea at my back.
Across the bridge a road leads
up the mountain. At the end of the road
is a logging landing overgrown with alders.
These mountains are plentiful:
iron pyrite and *quipus* of wire rope . . .

*Quipus*: knotted and twisted cords the Incas used to keep
accounts and record history.

# GRINDSTONE MOUNTAIN

Out of breath on the summit,
looking toward the Pacific
Ocean through the fog, I am
remembering the story of
an industrious man
on his way through these mountains
from Portland to Tillamook,
pack-horses laden with
grindstones—sorely needed—at
that moment. Here—right here—he met
another man coming up
with news that a ship
had arrived with grindstones:
with grindstones no longer needed
in Tillamook, he dumped
his whole cargo down the slope
of this mountain, where
I straddle the ridge.

# CEDAR BUTTE LOOK-OUT: 1953

Once inside the cedar shake cabin
I quickly climb the ladder, hoping
always to make some discovery, to
see something new from the view
point in the small cupola.

It is the first week of fire
season and I perform the ritual,
sweep up the fallen, the dead
flying ants.

Pausing from my task, I see the fading
silhouettes
enemy airplanes
tacked to the strips of window frames
around the dusty panes of glass.

They remind me of those other aircraft
of the 1940s, unsuccessful
incendiary bombs, floating
on the west wind from Japan, devised
to catch in the arms of tall firs—

We still stumble across them
in the woods: paper
lanterns rotting in the rain.

I see the ocean, to the west
over snag-covered ridge tops.

A buzzard circles the cupola—its shadow
not among the aircraft on those cards.

He takes his afternoon nap
perhaps dreaming of
those years

      —of highball
       logging with steam donkeys
       yarding wrist thick
       cables until they snap

      and felling Douglas fir
      by hand, with the bullfiddle,
      leaving stumps bigger around
      than the table in the cookhouse
      and smoother

      —of silver railroads, the only
       roads through the green virgin
       timber stands

      endless, the passing of the log
      trains down the toothpick trestles

      —of cork boots riddling
       hardwood dancehall floors
       on Saturday night . . .

Through the window toward Gold Peak
dog-hair stands of buckskin snags:
white haze along the ridgetops . . .

Now a camp cook in summer,
too old to do timber cruising,
painting road signs of roads he pioneered,

snoozing on August afternoons, on the army cot,
snow-haired, tale teller, old Tupper.

*Trask Guard Station*
*Fire Season 1952-53*

# THE KNOT

His dreams always had the scent
of cedar & pitch
bubbles in July not unlike the blisters
on his hands the first three weeks

work. Water from the rusty tin
cup at the spring beside
the road had its own taste, the animals
must have known that, the tear
drop shape of each half of the deer
tracks in the mud indicated
the popularity of that drinking

place. Spitting in the palm of his
hand extinguishing a cigarette
there a kind of concern for the woods

or lighting a cigarette in the 40 mph
wind, cupping his hands just so, drawing
once, just in the right way, a
skill, like rolling a smoke
on horseback, drawing the string
tight with the teeth on the pouch of
Bull Durham.

He had never done any of those
things, except, maybe, while
dreaming, instead he sharpened pencils,
unaware of the scent of cedar in

that. There is something in the smell
of wood, he thought, his life
somewhere in the grain

swirls of timber
bound log, left behind
like the eddies down be
low in the river.  Red

the word of wood
he would think
about it or better
dream it all night.

The next day he would wake
fatigued, go out looking
for the log with that
pattern or after the rain walk
the river bank
looking at the swirls.

Sees instead the small fingerling
salmon caught in the pot
hole carved out of shale by the past
currents, catches sight of the red
crayfish, scurrying backward missing
one claw, frightened by the shadow

He gives it up, goes back to the city
finding no answers
in the past, uncertain
of the future

Gives it all up
and searches in his dreams
for that pattern, that
swirl of light
around him like the grain of wood
flowing
around a knot.

Barney told me
at least once a week
"Don't get caught
in the bite of the line"
(old logger's warning
in steam donkey
high line logging).
While the logs were being yarded
to the tree one caught on a stump
and it was Barney
who hopped over the slack cable
to check the choker bell
just at the moment
it snapped tight—split
exactly
in half from the crotch
up.  Someone
went for his brother
who owned the company.
"Get back to work, you
loggerhead sonofabitch," the brother
said, "We'll take him in tonight
when this train of logs is loaded."
Lying in the shade
of the water tank
he waits for the evening
log train to Carlton
two halves
of a peeled alder log
turning red.

My uncle on his way home from town
late one night, walking the tracks . . .
As he was crossing  a trestle
he heard the train coming. He quick
hopped down and hung by his hands
from a railroad tie until the train passed.
Not knowing how far his feet were from the ground
he hung there like that the rest of the night.
At daybreak he discovered his feet were exactly
four inches from the ground. It made him
so goddam mad
he hung there until sundown.

If I say Hollywood, Beverly Hills, Dog Patch,
Trask Ranch, East Fork Camp and Timbuktu
you will understand, because you
as I did, lived and worked in those places.
The others will not, for they are thinking
of California, Al Capp and the Orient.
They do not know the Tillamook County
of the twenties, thirties, forties and fifties.
Or if they have heard those names
they will take out their maps and search
without finding and think me
just another name dropper.  Or when they
drive through the Coast Range, they will find only
rotting wood logs, a few snags, rusting tin cans.

Those names are on my map.
Fire, snow and rain have destroyed the signs
of settlements in these mountains.
In 1953 I searched for Timbuktu (it was on the
map then) and never found it.
Nor any gold or gold mines in a long winter
of prospecting and exploring.

And you, Tupper. I suppose
you are dead now. Certainly
the world at large
does not know you.  In some file
under the "T's" there must be an entry
that reads:  Milton Tupper.
Lumberjack, timber cruiser, cook,
road builder, log scaler, road sign painter.
There is a reason I am writing
you. Last week in Hoquiam

I saw something: a steam donkey,
on new skids, its boiler
painted bright red . . .
I thought of you and knew
you would be interested.

The part about the red boiler you will laugh
at, wherever you are.

Yrs,
Skip

P.S.    This is a poem which will be in a book
called *The Shingle Weaver's Journal.* That will mean
much to you.
You will say you have a poem for me.
We will both laugh at that one.

*from* NIGHTMARKS (1990)

Like four pages of darkness
he stood there unable
to speak. His foot gone to sleep,
his windless mind lost
on safari, he waited
for some event, wanted it
hoping his pen would run out
of ink or he could excuse himself.
But the moon was up (somewhere),
it was foggy, he didn't know what
time was, there were no excuses;
everything was real, there was no way
out of it this time. At least
the nylon stocking would protect
his identity. His face itched.
He had forgotten to shave
but they wouldn't mind —
he could do that later or they
would do it for him.

# L'AGE D'OR

## 1

We are all flag wavers, true;
or we are one river playing
the part of another
in a skit about two flags
having a sword fight.

## 2

Beneath the suit of armor
two skeletons dark with age;
one knight winks
at the other
using someone else's eye.

## 3

The horses grown old and
tired of waiting for the war
have gone off and bloated themselves
by the picture of a meadow

where a swollen brook
runs the wrong direction.

## AN EDITED VERSION OF THE FILM
## *ALL THAT TREMBLES IS NOT THE EARTH*
## STARRING ROBERT REDFORD

---

> *. . . A man  on his hands  & knees*
> *in the dark*
> *clutches something . . .*

Four cowboys play
cards sitting on dynamite boxes.
They have various rifles and shotguns
on their knees, they are waiting
for birds, Indians, or rustlers.
One of them drinks from a bottle,
another is reading the *Police Gazette*,
a third man who is not
wearing a cowboy hat is disinterested.
There is murder in his eye,
the card game is going badly for him,
the spots on the cards are developing
into animals (ibex, antelope, etc.).
At some point the cowboys are
so intent on the game they notice nothing.
An Indian walks by in a canoe, they see nothing.
Rustlers rustle by hiding steers
behind their skirts,
winking at one another
in a knowing way.
There is a circle around all of this,
a lariat of horsehair
to keep rattlesnakes out of the game.
From time to time
one flicks its tongue
in a daring move across the circle nobody
notices.

# TWO STATES

## 1

And on returning home he found her
lying still, as though asleep

and as he bent to kiss her
he noticed nipples
dissolving beneath his breath.

And her hair was withered
Straw—stubble burnt in preparation
for seeding.

       And for a moment
       he thought
of green grass, no
fields of waving wheat
(a fading image: for he never liked
extremes
in weather). Kansas.

## 2

The imagination is a wild thing
(again) he thought, her eyes
a rush of images in his mind
until an eyeball rolled away
down a cheek leaving a trail
in the dust.

He imagined he heard it splash
into the sea—years away
in Oregon.

The smell of water
soaked leaves,
        the repetitions
    of the police
    cars and curbs,

    a green cow
flying over the post office
    dropping leaves
        the size of
circus tents.
    Evening sky hangs
    in the background
    like a huge orange
tennis shoe.
        Now we know
it is autumn and why
        the cow
did what she did.

Who watches
white paint peeling
from the rocker
the east wind
rocks on the concrete
porch.

Who hears the radio
playing
from the camper-top
on blocks
in the alley.

Who sees
the smoke drifting
from his fingers.

Who remembers
between the crush
of lemon grass
and the last lines
of a song:

"With whiskey
for his pillow
he lay down,

he lay down."

# THE BIRCH PLYWOOD SKIN OF JUST POSSIBLY THE WORLD'S LARGEST AIRCRAFT DESPITE ITS NAME IS REALLY THE SKIN OF HOWARD HUGHES' SOUL AND WILL NEVER FLY AGAIN

The aging crew inside
has pasted on the inner surface of the soul
that no one sees
all the old newspaper accounts of
the disappearance of Amelia Earhart,
bogus last wills and testaments
of the unknown father of Hughes,
and all the remaining pin-up
calendars of Jane Russell.

On the floodlit dock
Jane Russell herself is waving to the crew,
brushing imaginary straw from her hair,
dreaming she is still every man's desire.
The barber stands beside her believing he has been summoned
here by some great and unknown power, holds his shears
at the ready, helpless and confused.
But another man, the designated killer
(dreaming the ultimate insect)
looks as though he had just knocked a giant
out of the air
as the soul of Howard leaves its skin
and floats off into the darkness.

# DEAD MAN'S CURVE

After all the years
when the road has been

moved, the curve
forgotten, and the pavement

bulldozed up,
along certain turns you will find

spots where the track still shows
and you can follow it

into humus
near the forest's edge.

Time was when he had time
to follow segments of old logging roads

to be lost in the deep forest snags
where the road runs out.

A white line runs through his life
now, what time does he have?

Eyes focused on the line,
following cars, what time does he have

for the deer
standing at the world's edge,

two lights shining back at him
from the darkness?

## RUST ON THE TRACKS FOLLOWS
## THE LAST TRAIN DOWN THE LINE

You'd like to think
he went on to greater things,
that he headed down to Peru
to run the narrow gauge railway,
that he died in a barroom fight
in Lima . . . but

Where angels guard the gates
at an intersection
he's buried, the engineer,
no railroad
crossing in sight.

His engine, old number
something or other
on another train
or truck for scrap
for the War

Effort, reincarnated
in Liberty ships,
in tins of food,
tines of pitchforks
and four generations
of Fords.

Here in this cut
the ties refuse to rot
into their place
in the cycle, but remain
as oily and crumbly
as the old elbow length
rawhide gloves he wore.

Go ahead, walk
the gradual incline. Behind you
the toothpick trestle
is only partially hidden by thirty years
of new trees.

How to get back
to the simplicity of it
—the skating
on the small pond, on thin ice—
where it was always possible
to break your nose
over a girlfriend
and live though it,
to get your heart broken
and get over it right then
and there.

Years later
things are not so simple.
Your head is a balloon
full of words, your fingers
something like honeyed batwings
(when they come to visit),
reality something
poking through on rare occasions
full of bones
on Sunday afternoon:
a plastic bag
full of chicken
but bones all the same
when the picnic's over.

# THE SEVENTH WAVE OF SADNESS

### 1

My tears stick to your cheeks
like the pitch from the pines
of Mt. Olympus.

### 2

Your presence hangs around me
like a summer cold
like the smell of blossoms
of the sour orange.

### 3

Your words are goodbye, goodbye, goodbye
falling like round sedimentary stones
unpeeling from the impact
syllable by syllable
layer by layer until the sandstone is sand
blown away
except for the one fine grain that falls
into my pocket.

### 4

The sun rises
the sun goes
the moon comes
a stone
against my heart.

He was always near the bridge
on the rusty road to Castillo Nuevo
wearing the beret faded
to something between transparent and limestone dust.
He would begin by saying *You do not understand me.*
*Until the time that you understand me*
*do not talk to me at all.*
He began each sentence with *You do not . . .*
The possibilities were endless, are endless
with such a point of view or shall we say philosophy.
He spoke with, rather in,
a lapidary language
such as one does not hear these days.
He was old. Well not
really old, just short.
Actually, he just stooped over
and you would swear sometimes he was talking
to his big toe.
He would talk to trees. To the river. To leaves
floating by. To rocks.
Sometimes he would talk to people
and whatever he talked about
he would begin each sentence with *You do not . . .*
People simply shook their heads
and walked away slowly
and sadly.

## THE FIRST WHITE BUTTERFLY OF SPRING / *LA PRIMERA BLANCA MARIPOSA DE LA PRIMAVERA*

*—for Kathy Romero*

Remembering the nameless creek running full;
the large Oregon ash beside the shack;
the plans, the tree, the fort our father
would not let us build in that tree;
the peculiar arched roof of the shack;
copper pennies or sixteen penny nails
laid flat on the nearby tracks
to be flattened by the logging train
that passed by in the morning or
rushed through the bedroom
at midnight, some nightmare
monster to become accustomed to.

~�—

On this Sunday spring morning
overlooking the city
the eye catches
barely a shadow, forgetting
the irregular flight
my eyes cannot follow, forgetting
the matter of days that is the life
of a butterfly.
By evening the sky clouds over
and the wind is blowing.

When I slip out of bed
and leave you there fast
asleep in the middle of the night
and travel to regions unknown
I walk through the dark
for hours simply counting
all the lights in the city.
Sometimes I see wonderful
strangers out there. But
the trains in the Brooklyn Yard
talk more, a tug whistle
on the river says more, the red lights
of radio towers beam out messages.
The people do no speak
to me, it's late
and night walkers are suspicious.
Sometimes here by the gate
I meet you
disguised as the neighbor
who at 2 A.M. is pruning
camellias. But I know it is you.
You are also the man down
on the corner
who lost a leg on moonlit
railroad tracks.

I know it is you
tonight
as you stand by the gate
of burnished brass
with letters in Latin
saying
*All who are homeless, welcome*

*to the City of Roses.*
And by this gate we join hands
and raise open palms
to check for rain.

Dawn shapes itself
into buildings—
we recognize the movie
house on the corner.
As we walk through sleep
we build a city
as familiar to us as rooms
in our own house.

# POEM SUGGESTED BY A LINE FROM THE IRISH POET OF LISCANNOR, AODH BUÍ MAC CRUITÍN

He sees the angry face of the sea
as though he has brought the *pucán* in

against the tide, making his way slowly
into Liscannor at night. Lights

missing for years, like the one at the end of the pier.

But he has the lights and eyes of years
going out at dawn, coming in at dusk.

The water is quiet now inside though
it is shallow and there is always danger.

Running aground the keel suddenly
scars the soft bottom sands.

He wakes in a sweat.
The boat tied to the bollard under the missing light.

*Pucán:* open boat, fishing smack.

A crow-black slate roof—
        there must be thousands
in Eire and England—
        square, weathered some-
times, tar-coated, steep-
        pitched over stone
houses.  The same
        soft rain flies from
over the Atlantic
        and falls, a murder
of crows exploding.

# AN IRISH POSTCARD: SCHOOLGIRLS
## WALKING BELOW KYLEMORE ABBEY

They scatter like geese,
As we walk up the lane, re-
form in a casual line
and mill down along the lake.

Up at the abbey after tea,
starched, white-bonneted nuns
watch through tracery
swans on the crystal lake.

In the background, the great wood
rises to watch over the abbey.
Beyond the woods, sentries:
the Twelve Bens.

But the schoolgirls,
in blue smocks and white blouses,
take their ease with Gold Flake
cigarettes as they walk down,

cross the Dawros that drains Kylemore Lake
and flows to the Atlantic,
where it bathes the shore
of Inishbofin, the island of the white cow.

The postcard shows
reflected in the mirror lake
the abbey and giant trees
(*Coil mhor*, the great wood).

What it does not reveal is
schoolgirls stealing away

to smoke, nor the white-thighed
girl on the lakeshore, bare feet dangling

in cold waters.

## UNDER THE BRIDGE ONE WOMAN FACES ANOTHER TO SPEAK OF RAIN OR EARLY EVENING

*It will be nice tomorrow,* she must be saying.

*The street is full of people coming and going,* the other says.

*As the sun is going, the moon is coming.*

Yes, her friend replies, *as sure as the ships leave for Barcelona in the evening . . .*

*. . . and return in the morning,* she says, turning
to search the sea
for her husband's red boat.

# WORDS OF THE EX-FISHERMAN TO HIS EX-WIFE

*This reef is always extremely dangerous, even*
*when winds are light and the sea otherwise calm.*

—*Boating in Coastal Waters*

From this distance in time and space
there remains a pencil sketch
of a reach of riprapped rocks,
the North or South Jetty where we went
with little thought
through rough bars to stormy seas
and returned each time to safe harbor.

I can hear faintly
the whistle, gong and bell
that mark the channel.

In the windowless night of years
I can still see Yaquina Reef
where the mast of a tuna boat stands
above the rocks,
its crow's-nest a warning
to me at least.

Though you have never seen these things
I wish you could have
or could take at least these words as warning.

*—for Bud Sullivan*

Out past the hundred fathom curve
at this hour sky waves bounce off
the ionosphere with tracings,
hillocks to confuse me, as I attempt
superimposing two mountains
that are not mountains
but Master and Slave: two
signals translated into
Loran lines tell me
we have arrived.

The ink line
printout of the echo
sounder, the bottom
profile, a scrawl rising
from the ocean floor: suddenly
the water
is barely seventy fathoms.

No sunken pirate ships
on this underwater island
guarded by dog-
fish among the mountains
of sea-green light
as I stare at the oscilloscope
in the darkness of the wheel house
at 4 A.M.

No treasure but Dover sole
lulled in these shallow waters
over Nelson Island.

# MAZARRÓN

In the patio of the Bar Royale
with friends recently met
we listen to the BBC
to catch details
from the rising and falling
newscast of yet another war in Israel
until some local fishermen
start playing the jukebox
and singing along with the Mariachis.

I ask them how they know
the Mexican music
and they come to our table
where we drink
long after the barman has gone
leaving us a bottle of Bacardí
and a lantern as our only light
in the blackness
that stretches 200 miles
to Algeria.

I turn to the glint
of two fixed bayonets.
Four of us are tourists
I explain to the *Guardia Civil*
and leave the fishermen
to speak for themselves.

They walk with us
toward our hotel,
whispering
the bar being British
is suspect, visible

from the beach, the lantern
could be a signal
to a boat offshore;
we could be smugglers, they laugh
when we get to the place
they have hidden their car.

# THE HILLS OF DISTANT LOVES LIE

*Easily, the hills of distant loves lie*
*beyond winter's light . . .*

—Keith Wilson
*In memoriam*

This will be moving.
This will be human
and out of this . . .

moon, stars.
Easily,
the hills of distant loves lie

behind Mary's Peak
and Table Top
Mountain.

If the fog lifts
this will be moving
this will be human

as the cry of the murre
looking for its infant
is not.

It is moving
as the sea
is moving.

And if the fog lifts at sea
there will be horizon,
the hills and beyond.

Distant loves
if the fog
lifts.

The cry of the murre
is too much
like our voices crying

at one another,
looking for something
lost in fog.

When the fog burns away
we expect
the sun.

And we are sure
the same distant
hills will be there, to the east.

And there will be sea
we will be able
to see for miles,

to look harder
for something lost,
moving

human
if the fog
lifts.

## MOON MULLINS

The first time I met him
we were headed out of Newport
for the Columbia Bar.

He came up to the dog house,
took out the chart
rule and a number four pencil,
drew a heavy line roughly north
and said this is the way we'll go boys
and disappeared below.

I think he once said
that the surface of the sea
was rolling hills green and sometimes
blue where goats or maybe he said boats
gamboled and frolicked
sometimes in the bright sunshine,
sometimes hiding behind waves in the fog.

And once I think I heard him call
the seaweed that collected on the lines
goatsbeard or maybe he was just mumbling
or maybe it was a bit untranslated
from his native language
whatever that was.

The thing I'm certain he said
the one thing he was right about
was that the ocean has a face
angry or smiling and you can read it
but you'd better read it right.

There is a valley between this house
and the light-sprinkled hills across the way.

There is a river or sea of darkness
and in between silhouettes of houses
like rocks to beware of.

The streets outside are empty
and quiet, the dog sleeps.

On the hill, in the house
the lights are left on
as though a warning:
shallows, sands
at the base of the hill.

We have stayed awake tonight
keeping the light and watch.

A tug whistles in the distant dark.
I think green starboard, red port.
What I see is the top of the bridge:
a single red light.

There are no ships in this place.

There is no danger out there
as the coffee,
as the night, gets colder.

# KALSKAG JOURNAL (AUGUST-SEPTEMBER, 1986)

*Kalskag, pronounced the Yupik way*
*sounds like bubbles*
*of air and blood*
*escaping the throat of a dying man.*
*The name means:*
*"elbow of the river."*

### SATURDAY

We walk the Paimut Portage Trail
toward Aryhymot Lake.

Here the Kuskokwim and Yukon
squeeze together and almost meet.
Glaciers have left teardrops:
lakes, sinkholes, ponds.

### SUNDAY

Late summer. Wind
blows the tundra grass and bog cotton.
Last year's smelt dry,
swaying with the iron Russian Orthodox bell
in the village.

Bottle flies worry diadems
around fish ready for smoking:
dried smelt for oil lamps, smoked salmon
and whitefish for the long
long winter.

Back in the bush I hear the bullfrog-
throbbing of a diesel on the river:

the *Tanana Chief*, bright blue
and white, three deck tug,
butts two barges up the Kuskokwim,
brings fuel
on the last day of August.

## MONDAY, LABOR DAY

10:30 P.M. I write this
as I sit out on the wooden steps of a cabin
designed by Russian priests.

Later, one light in the dark,
an anchor light: *The Chief*
rests on the river
above the village.

## TUESDAY

Once again the iron bell. It is not
the Angelus of noon or 6 P.M.
calling out, "Natalia, Melania,
Nicolai, Alexis, Ivan, Wassali
(of the Nooks, the Little Fish,
the Kameroffs, the Urovaks, the Epchooks):
Come, come and worship!"

The oddly proportioned cross
of alder
seems to bleed.

The dead bell rings again . . .

The priests, one Roman one Russian, follow
in procession

arm in arm
           ahead of one or two
pickups, one with the coffin in back;
and then the one-hundred-twenty five
villagers.

     The new Protestant
shopkeeper/preacher is lost
with the stragglers.

## FRIDAY

The aspen leaves are turning.
A red squirrel cuts spruce cones,
and the geese, fewer this year
head south.

Egg gathering is curtailed, fewer
geese for the table. This year
there are more swans and,
if things get tough, cranes.

Three items for a bush lunch:
smoked salmon,
rose hips,
and high bush cranberries.

Two Yupik words learned: *Chamai,* hello; and
*maggoya,* mosquito.

One grim riddle asks the difference
between a dog team and a snowmobile.
*The Yupik know:* you can't eat the snowmobile.

Four deaths in four days:
one infant, two elders,
an old man, someone's uncle.

 *from* A SUITCASE FULL OF CROWS

(1995)

*—for Amy*

After long hours of following
the arc of Lake Superior,
tired of scenery and mosquitoes,

we cross the border at Pigeon River
and stop at Grand Marais
for lunch in an antique shop.

The maiden aunts who run the place,
seeing children, take away china,
bring plastic plates.

Lake Superior is enough
of an ocean. You go looking for whales
with a long stick.

We buy chunks of lake ice,
kept all summer in sawdust barns,
for our cooler chests.

Long before the badlands,
the ice is dirty water,
you get sick on your brother.

It's Sunday in South Dakota,
all the bars closed,
no liquor. The whole

mean-streak, hung-over town
is on Main Street
dying for a drink.

In the café
they won't take our travelers' checks.
When we pay cash for our meal

we get change in hard looks
that follow us
most of the way home.

In the snow and fog
of the mountains in Yellowstone
your pregnant mother faints.

Your brother and I fish
in boiling water near Old Faithful.
I get my hair cut in Mountain Home, Idaho.

After the Craters of the Moon,
the rest is trying
to stay awake

down the Columbia Gorge
to Portland
where it's Saturday night.

And somewhere off the freeway
in the Dakotas
a lot of cowboys are drinking

and by noon tomorrow
they'll be red-eyed and thirsty
on the Main Streets of America again.

During those mornings cracked by the heat
after driving all night,
crumbly chunks of asphalt,
the oily taste after rain,
waiting for six-weeks grass to sprout along the highway,
he lights another cigarette.

By mid-afternoon the turns of the road shimmer:
Mirages when the yellow line has shifted—
*Cold Beer  Café  Eat Here*
with the blacktop melting . . .

Into the evening. Is the road still intact among the trees?
two dim headlights are his eyes,
a small and foreign car, he stares.
From the forest's edge a deer stares back at him.
stars watch, the moon
reflects in small oceans of leftover beer
splashing foam against Greek islands of shoulder gravel.

# BUS RIDE

Pretend you're on an airplane,
only it never leaves the ground.
It flies so low the lights outside
your window are towns you pass by.
Your airplane twists and turns
on a runway that never seems to end.

Take along a thick, boring book
to make you sleepy. Take along
a travel flask, it will help, pretend
the woman next to you is beautiful
and dying to talk . . .

Close your eyes. Before you know it
you'll be landing in your town.
It will seem as though something
close to the earth flew you
the whole way.

I pull off the highway—

Not the California
of San Francisco or L.A.,

but Likely, the progenitor of
bad puns.

A wild place, they say
during rodeo season.

*The Most Likely Café*
Most likely for what?

Is this where
as I sit sipping my Coors,
the girl of my dreams
will burst through
those double doors
to save my life?

*Not likely,*
thinks my reflection
in the long cracked Cape Horn
mirror behind the bar.

The bartender asks,
"Another one?"

# EARLY SPRING MORNING FLIGHT
# TO BETHEL

Among the few people
on the plane
are two girls
twin moons descending
from the darkness.

They speak Yupik:
you think
they are two white moons
conversing.

You won't believe
in two moons for the earth
but you are half
asleep.

Perhaps it is the sun
speaking to her brother
who has lost his fire.

It is two sisters
speaking of a cruel winter
of eating muskrats
and cracking bones of cranes,
of hunger.

You see below
the wafer-thin tapeworm
frozen to the brown belly
of the tundra.

The pilot tells you
it is the Kuskokwim River.

*Keles* are household spirits.

In bad novels the *keles* become good spirits.
In good novels the *keles* are bad spirits.

When things get tough
the people simply rise up to the skies
becoming stars
        and recognizable constellations.

       The real ending
       of many Yupik stories:

*. . . and then the buzzards come.*

# PIUTE

*—for Rich Blevin*

He has been to Rush Creek
near Mono Lake

gathering the old food
in the traditional way

for the old people
the *Ku-za-de-ka,*
the larvae eaters.

He shows me: *ku-za-vi,*
fly larvae skimmed
from the lake
(chewy, grainy,
with resiny aftertaste).

*Piaghi,* dried moth caterpillars
captured from the Jeffrey Pines

*Tu-ba-a,* piñon nuts
ground into meal
in a *metate.*

He says, "You try it
sometime."

The next day I find a note:
"*tu-ca,* to eat; i.e. eat"
(to encourage me).

Before you eat it, say something
good, like a little prayer.

Say, this *ku-za-vi* will be good for me,
something good will happen
if I eat this *piaghi*, etc."
I hesitate—

he pauses, laughs
his own full laugh
then says,

*You can say it in English.*

Just north
of Lost Horse

Plateau
on Ahtanum Ridge

beneath sagebrush
a sloughed rattlesnake

skin four feet long
is found by the wind.

At the entrance
to a quarry

a rancher's
boot kicks up

the face of a
Cherokee chief

from crushed rock:
one of two sides

of a nicked and scarred
coin of ironies.

In the chief's visage
etched the sadness

of *resettlement*
from Alabama, from Oklahoma,

the bison pressed to Earth
beneath the crush of illegal traffic,

trucks and cars passing
through the reservation

here
in this other country.

## POEM FOR 1992

Before we celebrate

genocide,
the theft and rape
of these continents,

dating from Amerigo Vespucci,
fraudulent cartographer,

let's ask the Great Spirit
or God or Allah or Yahweh
to forgive us.

Before we say
last rites
or Kaddish
over the big stumps,

let's ask protection
for the remaining elders, the surviving
witnesses:

sing a song
beginning with

*Sikwo-ya, Sikwo-ya*

or whatever words
we know.

## I

The flash of emerald green
in the black feathers of the magpie

(I'd not noticed in central Washington
or Ireland . . .)

I've seen many of those feathers
thought them only black

on what an Irish poet called
"half a white crow."

## II

I walk, finding game trails,
noticing deer tracks, grainy mounds
of harvester anthills, piles of pellets

as I make my shortcut through the desert
on my way home.

. . . The brittle, rent and broken sagebrush

fading tracks of tires in the sand

the detritus

a spot of snow in the shade
its imitation twin a shred
of styrofoam.

Nearby
a piston rusting, no, two
from some great machine failed . . .
Was this our civilization?


## III

Everyday as I walk here
each discard, each rusted pop bottle cap
and aluminum can more familiar.

Who could hold the desert
in such disregard? the wind
should whisper.


## IV

Last week snow left moisture
to feed bunch grass and bitterbrush
and rot, perhaps, newsprint fragments.

The setting sun, even in winter, tries
to fade the artificial color
of printed scraps
pushed along by the wind
as its sweeps the sand floor.


## V

The mule deer that gathered
around the Great American sage
this misty morning
have disappeared.

## VI

In the cerulean blue
six miles above the desert
not cloud but ozone-threatening
gas and heat, vapor trail of a jet
whose passengers see nothing below
but *earth tones*

                earth brown . . .
What lives down there?
they ask each other.

What could live down there?

Once when flying over the arctic ice
looking down on all that white,
I asked myself the same question.

# RETURN

## I

1954 and Manhattan Island
and the Statue of Liberty dissolve in mist.

The *U.S.N.S. Private William Thomas,*
a troopship, skirts Cape Hatteras
gale force winds and high seas.

>Four decks below the waterline
>the *riqueños* shoot craps
>smoke White Owls
>until by midnight the deck is awash
>in vomit, until the 38th Parallel is a bad dream
>and every approaching island
>is Puerto Rico.

>Guantánamo is not San Juan
>but they are ready
>when it comes into view.

## II

On the deck at sun-up flying fish
are thrown back into the Caribbean:
Trinidad and Tobago
left astern
like the khaki overseas caps we throw down
to waving and cheering women and children
on the dock at the naval base
in Port-of-Spain.

>The thin G.I. from Caracas is sick
>on the stack of hammocks

pale from *mal-de-mer* or celebration
since Cuba, as our ship slides
between postage stamp islands and Venezuela,
He does not come to the rail
to see, twenty miles from shore,
the Orinoco's coal black fan
of thin savannah soil
suspended in sea water,
waving its welcome to him.

## III

At nine degrees north of the equator
Panamá's *selva* waits

for our *latino* brothers
the Latin American School,
Eisenhower's nursery
for Peron's elite
and Somoza's troops;

for us the Jungle Warfare Center
to prepare us
for yet another war
in similar latitudes,
a place we then called
French Indochina.

# FINDING MIRAFLORES

*—for Ted Taylor*

## I

Stories of a Coca-Cola bottle full
of gold dust taken from a mine
in the late 1940s;
two yellow flakes in a vial of water
and a badly drawn map
got us here.

Lost, we avoid
the trees, the spines
of the black palm.

Our fear: the dark,
a blackness of the insides
of clothes closets,
filled with metal
sounds. Springs wound,
spoons clicking.

Close by we hear
the beginning—drops
of water from cup to
leafy cup—of what will be
the Río Negro.

We know not to drink
its sallow water
or wade its channel
but follow it down.

## II

The stream leads us
into a clearing
on the banks
of Miraflores Lake.

Away from shore
Barro Colorado
Island of red clay.

In last light,
a stalking
cayman alligator,
a *cayuco*, glides to shore.

Two hunters
disembark.

The design clear:
*montuno* hats,
silver moon edge
of sharpened machete,
shotgun barrel.

The rare European red hind
twists, slowly half-backs
into protective vegetation.

## III

On the other shore
of Miraflores
children sleep

on stomachs empty
as five gallon cooking oil tins
used to store rain water.

They dream of raindrops slipping
from ochre horse banana leaves,
of plates heaped with rice.

In the background luckless fathers
smoke homemade pipes
of Barro Colorado clay.

*Panamá*
1955

**I**

Like on the *African Queen*
the pitted smokestack leans,

the wooden hull teredo-riddled,
the anchor chain rusted to orange.

There the similarity ends.

No boozy Bogart aboard,
no sunburned, bonneted Hepburn . . .

A renegade *colombiano*,
the captain, his garrison cap
won at dice
from some American sergeant,
his first mate a Kuna Indian
in cutoffs and tee shirt.

The captain offers
to sell us pieces-of-eight,
a Spanish conquistador's cutlass.

**II**

We are thinking of women
in lacey *polleras*, dresses fanning
the humid night, laughing in balconies
across the isthmus
in Panamá
as we dive in cerulean
Caribbean waters
for lace-shot sea fans.

## III

After we have forgotten
soulful *morenitas*
and tepid Panamanian rice beer,
the acrid aroma
of sea fans
ripped from coral
will bring back
the Archipelago
of San Blas.

Stretching back,
back through time
to the jungle trail

into a sun spot
a break in the canopy
the fer-de-lance
like a rope

down the log
all neck—a living
shepherd's crook

eyes me
as I almost step.

Chance may
be the difference
between my survival
and his.

But twelve gauge
brass bound
shotgun
cartridges

Ants.

Monsoon rains.

Then dice
you can gather up
and drop
into your shirt pocket.

*Panamá*
*1955*

# FIELD, BURNING

The cinnabar moon
ignored the burnt stubble,

eyes of fire
across the creek.

Ignored the tall boy and the woman
on the other side of the mountain

tobogganing over slick wheat straws,
the bearded field whispering.

Ignored the two men, drinking
cheap brandy on the porch, remarking

on the full moon.

Ignored him as easily as
she had forgotten him.

It was September when she left.

That year it was in the particulate air,
love disappearing

in the updrafts, in black billows,
with burnt straw

and unwanted insects.

At the side of the road
in his old truck

he killed the lights,
watched the black fields

alone with the spotlight moon
and the chalky, smoky air.

# THE PENNED-UP WILD HORSES
# AT HALLELUJAH JUNCTION

Within the juniper and lodgepole pens
they look small as they dance
and shuffle in the frosty morning.

Waiting. Rounded up to be adopted
by teen-aged riders in Oregon. Others
driven into box canyons, loaded up
and trucked to slaughterhouses.

Do we curse the BLM? The Spaniards
who brought them here 300 years ago?
The original Americans who cut them loose?

This living symbol of the Old West
is crowding itself to extinction in the desert
as we fill it with our houses
and suck the springs dry.

The eagle and the mustang automobile logos,
is this the way we remember them?

Better to let the wild mare starve,
with freedom's full desert moon in her eye, or
turn her into a pet?

A few flicking tails, small
bursts of dust kicked up, the mustangs
neighing, unheard by us inside
the bus that passes at 55 M.P.H.

The bald eagle gone in a flash
on this January morning,
as a vigilant pale
rock-washed moon
falls behind the Sierras.

Along furrows, plowed contours
where later this spring

wheat will sprout where
east wind will whip dust

into devils where
bluebirds will arrive.

Nearby is the cold silhouette
of a John Deere. It pulls

small satellite moons
half-buried in the earth

of Horse Heaven's
high plateau.

Tonight
the coyote hesitates . . .

drawn toward
the sole street light he silvers . . .

I steal from my doorstep
for a better look

until I stand where he was
beneath the cone of misty light,

imagine him ranging outward
in ever widening circles.

I go back
to my trailer for more news

from Richland-Kennewick
where tonight people lie

in fitful sleep
dreaming of Chernobyl.

I am left with that
and a canopy of stars

distant as the Ukraine
as I turn out my light.

*April, 1986*

# I PRAY FOR PEACE IN THE NUGGET
## AS THE MIDDLE EAST WAR BREAKS OUT

Mid-afternoon, a late lunch,
my stomach flipping. The zombies
at the one-armed bandits have not seen sleep
or the news in days.

Across the aisle
a young mother breast feeds her baby,
looks over and smiles.

Has she heard the news?

She finishes and leaves. A few minutes later
she passes by the window, turns and smiles again.

I make up scenarios: she's stuck here
looking for work and a friendly face,
her husband has left her, she can't work
until the baby's older . . .

I try to pray but the only prayers I know
are blessings over bread and wine. I feel
like an exile, like an Arab might feel being here.

The Baptist Church billboard asks
*Have we read Revelations?* I ask have we
read history? Two American flags whip
the sides of a 4 x 4 as it roars down Highway 395.

I want the young mother to return
smiling, me smiling back, sure of a peaceful world
for her baby to grow up in . . .

As I pay for my meal, the cashier crows
*We've declared War!*
I rise up in the middle
of this tourist casino,

say blessings over bread and wine,
call out above the madness
and noise of gambling machines
to the cashier, the grandparents, parents, aunts and uncles:

We have *not* declared war!

# CANYON ECHOES

## I

That crack
is it an avalanche? A stick
of dynamite detonated?
Echoes up the canyon—
then silence
broken by the bugling
of Tundra swans overhead.

Then at my feet
water piping
from melted snow
on rock's edges
points to sandy ground,
to ditches
to creeks
over scree and boulders
to lakes
overflowing
to rivers reaching

the sea.

## II

The echo of empty oil drums
across deserts
of scorpions bigger than sparrows.

Winds of fire
oceans of fire.
What drips from broken
tanks and piping

whose death sound is so slick
and smooth
you can't hear it?

## III

Listen in the cool morning
for snow beginning to melt
when water comes in precious drops
and glistens
on the perfect diamond of a boulder,

hear it hit
pine-needle duffed ground,
follow it to the creek

to the river.

Carry it with you
to the Pacific —
remembering what the word means —

Pray for peace.

# BEARING WALLS

*—for Elizabeth*

## I

Just how much
will the walls
of love bear?

If we remove
traditional support, uprights,
what header
of what density, of
what strength
of feeling
to support the sky?

Can we figure love's live weight?

Perhaps
feelings don't weigh as much
as footfalls in an upstairs room.

## II

What we have
does not require
a house
of such sturdiness

to hold it up
and in.

Let's build ours
of blue sky, southwest wind
a grain or two
of beach sand, a house

where a goldfinch
can fly through,

where morning's
sun in the east
can light us,

where we can look out
at mountains.

*from* AT THE EDGE OF THE
WESTERN WAVE (2004)

# A SENTENCE OF THE FIRST SOUNDS
## OF IRELAND

In Limerick City,
just off the transatlantic plane,
displaced in time, half-awake, tucked
beneath the cool blankets of St Rita's
in the blackness before dawn,
I hear stealthful footsteps
approaching below, the rattle
of glass bottles on the stoop—
then the clip-clop of horseshoes
and the sizzle of hard rubber tires
on the wet pavement,
as the milkman's delivery van
resumes its route
through rainy darkened lanes
along the Ennis road.

# WALKING HOME LATE FROM CAHIRDERRY

*—for Michael Vaughan*
*In memoriam*

The guiding caravan lamp
in the small window
has long since guttered out.

Our toes in Wellingtons
don't feel the rutted road
somewhere beneath mud and sod.

Sally bushes and whitethorn
have closed in. Two cannot walk
abreast—we are three

in this velvet bag of four A.M.
Blackberries like fingernails
reach for cheeks and eyes.

He spoke of a ghostly coach-
and-four that traveled the *boreen*
on the right, up the hill

after midnight. Many claim
to have seen it.

In dead winter, late
after the hearth dance
in the cottage where we met,

the rain has stopped.

We say goodnight,
though it is nearer morning.

Suddenly a white horse
bolts from a roadside hedge,
dragging the block

it's hobbled to, like a head.
We turn into our place,
jingling the keys.

*Good Luck, again!* says
our new friend. He leaves us,

walks on down the road
toward the mass grave
of Killaspuglonane.

*Boreen:* a narrow lane.

# THE TEETH OF A RAKE ON
# A MAKESHIFT FORGE

As he laid the peat fire
around the hay rake
did I suppose
the unrusting of teeth important?

What image in that fire?
I said teeth, did I mean
bones, the mass grave of
Killaspuglonane so near . . . ?

I assumed the farmer
would use those parts
to save some other machine,
forgot the horses he owns
no longer pull the plow, the harrow.

The reddening teeth
are loosened by the heat
and pulled from sockets.
Did I say bones? The farmer
is bones, skin and bones, we say.
Lost his years and teeth.

⌒

Like the plodding steps
of the Percheron that sleeps
beneath the hill,
from foam barely visible
on an ocean three miles away,
the tide of darkness comes.

Ashes and hot coals
all that remain
of the makeshift forge . . .

The teeth of the rake
have become ribs
leaned against a stone wall.

Did I say ribs? Did I say
eyes winking in the ashes,
the cold earth, the night,
the soft rain . . .

# IN THE POST OFFICE TEARS PILE UP, UNOPENED

—Marieve Rugo
*If In Your Country*

He still works at the grain elevator
in Topeka. Pushes a grain shovel

all week, drinks away Saturday,
goes to late mass on Sunday.

She never heard from him,
for these twenty-some years a spinster.

He emigrated to America, was
to send for her when he got settled.

In 1949 he wrote he'd found work,
would send her passage.

But the village postman was given to drink
and forgetful. When he died in 1971

the shocked villagers found
dozens of letters stashed

behind the desk, slipped into corners.
Her long awaited letter like the rest

Undelivered, unopened . . .
Sean's address in America blurred

from the damp of the Post and Telegraph.
Maeve's name faded from his memory

by the Kansas sun.

# TIME

In a village of less than eight hundred
between half eleven and eleven forty five

from Griffin's, Blake's, MacLysaght's,
Curtin's, O'Harten's, Nagle's, Vaughan's.

Stack's, Hynes', O'Malley's, Keane's, Marrinan's,
Cullinan's, Considine's, Hayes', Kilmartin's,

McMahon's, Burke's, Crowe's . . . Phil's Place
(and a dozen or so with no name at all)

they walk, stagger, careen
and crisscross the cobbled street.

Few leave in cars. One or two try for a lift
with the Guard. Most are on foot.

One, apparently lost, sits on the kerb
by the Church of Ireland.

At the end of the street, past street lamps,
the last notes of a song, silence.

By midnight not a soul to be found.

*—for Gail Sherman*

These stone walls
across fields

up rock slopes of mountains.
A maze you said

millions of rocks
on and under

the surface
and a few magic stones

somewhere out there
in The Burren.

And a magic gate
in each stone wall

if you get on your horse
and ride

in just a certain direction.
Or maybe

you follow the white
cow as she steps through

the stone wall
into the twilight.


*Killaspuglonane, Co. Clare*

# CONNEMARA PONIES

Night here is a gate
opened into the field
and into me . . .

    *A distant*
    *thundering of hooves*
    *of the Atlantic*
    *surf at Lahinch*
    *comes through*
    *mixed with the sound*
    *of real thunder*
    *with southwest*
    *wind and hail*
    *stones striking*
    *the window panes*
    *of a cottage*
    *in the west of Ireland.*

In Portland,
Oregon, the weather
has warmed, ice on
the roof is melting,
rain dripping on tin gutters,
galloping Connemara ponies.

Tents of many colors pitched
on what there is of field beside the shore.
Cars from France, and caravans
park on the slotted slabs
and scoured out bowls
of carboniferous limestone.
"Return to Aran Five Pounds," says the sign
as though one could so easily return
to the Arans, call back the past.

How things have changed and how they have not.
The same battered and pensioned out
currachs lie upturned, tied
to the rocky ground, their hulls
facing the other great ocean, the sky.

Fog thickens across the Arans.
On a trailer near a fisherman's shed
a new *currach*.
In its shallow stern bilges
traces of sea water and riff of
sea-weed tell of the day's fishing.

Rough oars waiting for the big salt-cured hands,
ready to fish again.
The tarred canvas skin of the hull shines black.
The ribs are arched just so.
Towards the bow the shearwater
bends, at just the right angle
for taking the waves.

A vessel as finely made
as any now or in the past.

Cars and caravans will come,
campers strike their tents
and move on to other summers,
but this boat, as sure as the one
St. Brendan sailed

across the Atlantic to America, this *currach*
will slide down the ramp at Doolin Quay,
cross the first combers, swing around Crab Island
into the South Sound and fish forever here
between the shadows of the cliffs and Inís Oír.

1

On an island,
one spends time
learning to say
in two or more languages
*I am not in a hurry.*

2

On some islands
the quickest movement
is the passage
of money from one hand
to another.

3

The thought of a hand-
ful of dried corn
or coins hitting a tin roof
is one way of looking
at the rain.

4

*Several generations*
*of fishermen,* the woman sighed,
*have drowned in less,*
taking the two empty glasses
from the two empty men.

# THE HALF TOWER

*And angry shadows fighting on a wall*
*That now and then sent out a groan*
*Buried in lime and stone,*
*And sweated now and then . . .*
*Big drops that looked yet did not look like blood.*

—Edwin Muir
*Then*

That an IRA explosives practice
in the early 1920's only split
the Norman keep—here since
the 14th Century—leaving half of it
still standing over Liscannor Bay,
attests to the strength of the mortar,
whose cohesiveness derives from
the generous portion of blood
of oxes according to the local myth.

Stories are often heard
of the builders secretly
burying whole animals, arms, legs
hands in walls for good luck,
to appease old gods.

Were the master mason's thumb nail
to glint from the tower's
full green ivy cape in the setting sun

or a baby's cry heard on the sea wind
that drives ghosts through windows,

tonight, in the moonlight,
while the tower's recumbent other half
withdraws, crawling stone by stone
to the Delagh River,
who in Catholic Ireland
would believe it?

# HALF ISLAND

> *Newspaper headlines*
> *older than tea*
> *. . . there is a funeral*
> *in Lahinch*

### 1

Orange
ashes from burnt turf
rush out
to cover the heads
of those in mourning
those passing
to a funeral in Lahinch.

### 2

*He passes the well*
*below the valley-o*
*& green grow the lilies-o*
*bright beneath the bushes —*

O the whole sky
when she was in love
with this guy
when she was young
was there loving
in Lahinch.

### 3

She runs to the window
of the half-ruined tower

and drops down
autumn leaves
like yellow ashes
from the turf
fire scattered by the sea
breeze over the mourners
passing.


4

The farmer in black
wool suit walking
along the walled road
as he returns home
from a funeral in Lahinch
at twilight hears
the cuckoo singing
pauses to count
his remaining days.


5

The wind blowing
day after day
across the low hills
of County Clare,

the women flowing
month after month
behind white
washed cottages.

The tide ebbing & flowing
the beach, the
black beetle currachs head for
the open sea.

# LAHINCH

*The sea-breeze is at every door*
*and the sea at the end of every street*

—St. John Perse
*Strophe*

On that last night in Ireland
I watched spray from the waves

hit the lights high on the lampposts
along the promenade.

The port is Liscannor three miles up the road,
where a Wexford trawler slipped in

ahead of the southwester and slept
in the quiet water behind the quay.

You were not here with me then
I was a different person, arguing

mostly with the telly or myself in Kenny's
over fishing rights, Ireland's

fifty mile limit, not knowing my own
but loud as the storm anyway

after the pints of Guinness.

The red-faced publican, fair play to him,
nodded agreement about the fishery

locked the front door lowered lights
let his lone customer stay past time

glad for the grumbling
conversation against the winter night,

then ushered me out by the side door
once the Guard had passed.

The others had left the coal fire long since
gone out into the gale for homes

to dead grates, cold ashes in the hearth.

## LAMENT FOR THE MAN WHOSE AIM IS GOOD

There is a hole
In the breast of the wild pigeon
An irregular round hole
Burnt at the edges as though
The pigeon were a paper
Silhouette target and someone
Has made that hole with
The end of a burning cigarette

You could see daylight
Through that hole
And the glint of metal in the sun
A rifle maybe a man
Holding that rifle sighting
Down the barrel his aim is good

As the pigeon perches
For an instant on a wire
That forms an artificial horizon
Across the view out the window
The wire is high tension electric
Or telephone line

The pigeon is gone
The empty wire sings in the wind
An ancient melancholic air
A lament for the man
Whose aim is good

# SECURITY, CENTRAL BELFAST
## RAILWAY STATION

How does he know
who to search?
What does he read
in the eyes
while I read headlines?
I search each face too,
each pair of eyes.
Reflected there,
the security man smokes slowly.
Outside a raw September wind.
A desert dust works
into the eyes,
dust of what used to be
a church — sanctuary
for an armored personnel carrier.
Check-point:
soldiers move
through mazes,
rifles
at an indifferent
angle of readiness.
The security
man's fingers
tap out
a military tattoo

against wood.


*Belfast / Dublin / Killaspuglonane*

## COGADH / WAR

I

We shouldered
logs of deal and oak
because they told us to.

Carried the logs
across  mountain and bog,

while our horses ran
away to the sea
stood in the tide
their large marble eyes
blinded by the setting sun.

We horsed the logs
across rivers through glens
toward some center
agreed upon beforehand.

We packed the logs
through fine soft days
through gale and fog.

Until we encountered War
or maybe simply other men
like ourselves through beardless,
with swords long
as *currach* oars.

We dropped the logs
went no further.

These strangers
in tones guttural
compelled us to do so
or so we thought.

We lay down between the logs
looked to the heavens
and waited to die.

## II

With trying irons years hence
they probe and dig with slane.

They find few collar bones
or skulls—no crosses,
no racks of antlers
of giant Irish elk,

but oak and deal
ancient pieces of wood
put to one side in the drying wind
made into crude appliances
agricultural or birthing beds

or burnt with sods of turf
on nights of crackling frost
beneath the Plough and Stars.

Along the Antrim Coast
near the Giant's Causeway

a military helicopter sinister
purple in the photograph we took

worries the ragged coastline,
while ashore the dog patrols

the hedgerows as for game.
The hunt is for a man—

Says the news gone missing.
Above the Atlantic

up on the hill
a black bicycle waits,

leans toward a stone wall
towards breaking waves.

1

Where the Delagh runs
into Liscannor Bay,

from under the bridge,
we shovel silica,

laced with sea salt,
into bags and head south

along the coast
to a stone cottage

in Letterkelly.

2

A mistake
beach sand

for plaster,
but evocative.

The orange stain
comes through the years

of turf soot.
Above the hearth

the sea weeps
when the fire is hot.

We sometimes mixed
a bit of spittle

into the plaster
for luck.

And no doubt
a bit of blood

and sweat.

3

But there's no saving
the hearth.

Cracks appear
through the whitewash:

the battle here
dampness and heat.

The man who kept
the steady fire

John Haran
long since gone

to Moughna,
where the sheep

do a bad job
of keeping

the grass down
between stones

broken and tilting.

Desperate for shelter
from the pelting rain
I spotted the ruin.

I leaned the bicycle
against the wall,
the hearth would do me.

An ancient piece of bog
big as a whale's rib
over my head.

No one has sat
in this hearth
for forty years.

I hold my hands
where the fire
would be blazing.

The timber beam
had not been enough,
so someone added

the wedge of stone,
huge lintel to support
the black chimney, the sky.

# WATER CLOCK UNDER CURROCH O'DEA

### 1

The fog is all around us
and lately we've been burning coal
with our turf.  Our neighbor notices
the blue smoke from the white chimney,
says our cottage looks like a ship
steaming through fog
over the bog headed
into the wind.

### 2

On the hill
    in the distance
through Mary Green's field
                the path
shines like a river
    in the failing light.

It is as through
    I see us for the first time
though we have crossed
            this bog
countless times—
       tonight
the film stops
    we begin to see us
a frame at a time
    until
in one long line
    we fill the path.

3

After a sudden shower
the sky clears
full moon shines through
Sitka spruce.

All the meadows
tonight appear white
as though frost had come
a warning
that Fall is here.

It starts in August
and it is cooler now,
the nights longer,
winter before you know it.

# PADRAIC'S POEM

Inside Leary's ruin,
The cast iron bed remains,
A clump of Scotch thistles
Grows up between the springs.

Supplied with more than ample rain
And sun—the thatched roof gone
For years. Tonight it is the home
Of a young bull, a two year old,

Who watches us pass by his place
Below on the muddy road.
He stands, white face,

Content, silent, ignorant,
His head half out the window,
His hind hooves in the marriage bed.

I get up three times to check
the full moon's rise, hoping
to see it waddle like a fat red goose
across the back of Mt Callan
as it did the last night
of July.

By one A.M. the sky is a cave
of bare suggestions, bones
of light where the moon should be.

At three in the morning
a zig-zag
reflection of lightning
passes between the horns
and follows the horizon
of a grey cow's back.

By four a milk river flows
across the *slieve*
to The Blaskets.

*Slieve:* mountain.

## CAOINEADH

His grief is
like the soft rain;
the last petals
of ditch roses
along the dike;
the oily liquor
that seeps away
from the black turf banks.

He thinks of the collie,
Sam Óg, gone rambling,
never to return;
the pied wagtail
his cat brought
and left
on the stoop;
the cuckoo's lost
uncounted call
along the bog
in May;
the sweet full aroma
woodbine
on a close July night
as he walks the county road.

Brigid is gone sure
as the corncrake
is gone.

The rusting bedstead
borders
the sadness of dreams.

He carries his grief with him,
the stones he takes away
from the ruin
to build the wall.

It surrounds him
like a fire poorly laid
with turf that smokes
but won't catch fire.

Like peat sods spread on the bog
in a desperate wet season,
his grief begins to settle
back into the cold dark earth.

*Caoineadh:* the elegy or lament sung at an Irish wake. Keening.
*Sam Óg:* Young Sam

# FUNERAL IN MILTOWN

Dark into winter,
light into spring . . .

The cuckoo counts
days in the May evening.

Bridie, the hairdresser,
gone at forty from a tumor.

The doors of shops,
public houses . . .

Main Street closing
before the procession

as it trudges
from the funeral parlor

past the Garda Siochana
up to the church;

doors re-opening
as the cortege passes;

the wind fingering
the pages of a missal.

# WALKING ALONG THE HILLS ABOVE CLOONANAHA AT DUSK

The beauty of what once
was more than symmetry and form,
these stone walls
go with us, along roads
and sidehills, up mountains
and down into valleys,
holding in the lives
of cattle and sheep
and the man
in the worn grey wool suit
who comes to count
the animals or to drive them
home. And the woman
who comes with the tin pail
along this pathway to milk,
the dog with her
snapping at the hooves
and dewlaps of the cows.

At dusk I pause and look back
over the meadow toward Mal Bay
listening hard for the story
of these walls, hearing only
the slightest whisper
as I pass,
leaving them to settle
into the centuries
as sure as people settle into beds
at dark along these bogs.

As I clamber over this wall
one stone falls, complaining

with clattering song. Reaching for it
I start to replace,
stories told well,
the stone that comes to hand.